BROTHERS IN HOPE

THE STORY OF
THE LOST BOYS OF SUDAN

BY MARY WILLIAMS

ILLUSTRATED BY R. GREGORY CHRISTIE

Lee & Low Books · New York

To all the children of Africa—M.W.

Dedicated to all the children of the world affected by famine, poverty, illness and ignorance—R.G.C.

Acknowledgment
Special thanks to the Mays family and Valentino Achak Deng

LEE & LOW BOOKS Inc., 95 Madison Avenue, New York, NY 10016
leeandlow.com

Manufactured in China

Book design by Tania Garcia
Book production by The Kids at Our House

The text is set in Gill Sans
The illustrations are rendered in acrylic

10 9 8 7 6 5 4 3 2 1
First Edition

Library of Congress Cataloging-in-Publication Data

Williams, Mary.
  Brothers in hope: the story of the Lost Boys of Sudan / by Mary Williams; illustrated by R. Gregory Christie.— 1st ed.
    p. cm.
  Summary: Eight-year-old Garang, orphaned by a civil war in Sudan, finds the inner strength to help lead other boys as they trek hundreds of miles seeking safety in Ethiopia, then Kenya, and finally in the United States.
  ISBN 1-58430-232-1
  [1. Refugees—Fiction. 2. Self-actualization—Fiction. 3. Orphans—Fiction. 4. War—Fiction. 5. Sudan—Fiction.] I. Christie, Gregory, 1971- ill. II. Title.
PZ7.W66699Br 2005
[Fic]—dc22
                                                                        2004020965

▶▶▶▶ AUTHOR'S NOTE ◀◀◀◀

I first became aware of the Lost Boys of Sudan in January 2000 while working for the International Rescue Committee, a refugee resettlement agency charged with helping newly arriving refugees adjust to life in the United States.

I had lived and worked in two African nations and had some knowledge of the troubles that Sudan was experiencing. I knew Sudan was the largest country in Africa and that it was embroiled in one of Africa's longest-running civil wars—a war that had been raging on and off since the mid-1950s and was based on religious, political, and economic conflicts. What I did not know was that more than two million people, the majority from southern Sudan, had lost their lives in this war.

I was also shocked to learn that during a period of renewed fighting in the mid-1980s, approximately thirty thousand southern Sudanese children, many under ten years old, were forced on a trek of nearly one thousand miles in search of refuge. They came to be known as the Lost Boys of Sudan.

I founded The Lost Boys Foundation in August 2001 to increase awareness about the Lost Boys and to raise funds for them to access educational opportunities in the United States.

Before meeting any of the Lost Boys, I assumed they would be hardened and embittered by their experiences: the loss of their parents, near starvation, and exposure to violence, persecution, and deprivation. Imagine my surprise when the first group of ten young men walked into my office with huge smiles on their faces and excellent manners. They spoke English well and were quick to laugh. It was obvious they felt blessed to be given the opportunity to come to the United States.

When I asked one young man how they had endured such an arduous journey, he simply smiled and said, "It was the grace of God." The Lost Boys' unrelenting faith in God, their loyalty to one another, and their desire to acquire an education to better themselves and their country is a powerful testament to the strength of the human spirit.

This book is based on the true story of the Lost Boys as told to me by the young men who lived it.

Mary Williams
Founder
The Lost Boys Foundation

I was born in southern Sudan. I lived with my mother and father, grandparents, and two sisters in a small mud-and-thatch house. We were considered wealthy because my father owned many cattle.

As a young boy, I was frightened of these big animals.

"I am too small to care for such big animals!" I cried when my father told me I would have to learn to tend the cattle.

My father just smiled. "Garang, be brave," he said. "Your heart and mind are strong. There is nothing you cannot do."

When I turned eight years old, I began to tend some small calves on my own. I cleaned them, nursed them when they were sick, and led them to the very best pastures and watering holes. I quickly grew to love these animals.

Then one day everything in my life changed.

I was far from home tending my animals when my village was attacked. I could hear bangs like thunder and see flashing lights in the distance. Suddenly an airplane was circling above. Clouds of dust rose from the ground and bullets began to rain down on my herd. Many of the animals were killed. Others ran away in fear.

My throat and eyes were full of dust, but I found my way to the forest, where I hid in the shadows of the trees.

When the storm of bullets passed, I ran back to my village to find my family, but everyone was gone. The houses were burning and everything was destroyed.

I began to wander down the road, and soon I met other boys who could not find their families. We began to search together. As we walked, we met more boys on the road.

At first there was just me—one.

Soon one became many.

Too many to count.

Before war came, I had never seen so many people in one place. My village had only one hundred people. Now I was in a moving village with thousands of boys.

Like me, the other boys were away from their villages tending their cattle when war came. The adults and girls had stayed behind.

Some of the boys were only five years old. The oldest boys were not more than fifteen. We were children, not used to caring for ourselves. Without our parents we were lost. We had to learn to take care of one another.

The older boys decided to have a meeting.

"We must work together if we are to survive," one of the boys said. "We will form groups and choose a leader for each group."

"Garang Deng!" someone yelled. My name!

I had been chosen to lead a group of thirty-five boys. I was proud but scared. I knew how to take care of animals, not boys, but I did not want to let my fear keep me from helping my brothers. Then I remembered what my father had told me: Garang, be brave. Your heart and mind are strong. There is nothing you cannot do.

I joined the group of leaders, and we decided we would walk to a country called Ethiopia. Before war came to our villages, many of us had heard our elders talk of Ethiopia. They had said Ethiopians would provide a safe place for Sudanese running from the war.

Some of the older boys knew we must travel east to reach Ethiopia. It was very far and the journey would be dangerous, but it was our only hope.

We decided it was best to walk at night and sleep in the forest during the day to avoid soldiers and the severe heat of the sun. Many argued that it was too dangerous to walk at night because of animals hunting for food. After much talk we agreed that the soldiers and their warplanes were more dangerous than the animals.

We also decided that the older boys would adopt younger boys who couldn't care for themselves. I chose a little boy in my group named Chuti Bol. He was only five and cried for his mother.

The next evening we found the road to Ethiopia. We were glad to have a full bright moon, but it was still very dark. To make sure we did not lose anyone, each boy held the hand of the boy in front of him. Chuti was too small to walk long distances. I often carried him on my back. Everyone was tired and hungry, but no one complained.

There were a few boys in my group who knew how to find wild fruits that were good to eat and others who could hunt wild birds. Some days we had food to share, but most days there was no food to be found. We often ate leaves and bark from trees.

Finding food was not the only problem. Many days it was hot and dry and we were very thirsty. Sometimes we had to drink our urine to get moisture in our bodies. There were times when we got very sick. We made sure to rest often so the weaker boys could keep up.

We did many things to help us forget our hunger and our aching bodies. We played games and told stories. We made animal figures from mud, mostly cattle. I told Chuti how I used to care for calves. He was so impressed, he insisted I sculpt a herd of cattle for him. I was glad Chuti liked the cattle, even if they were just made of mud.

One evening as we were walking on the road, I heard Chuti crying. I picked him up and asked what was wrong.

"I'm scared you will leave me like my mother and father," Chuti sobbed.

"Chuti, your mother and father did not want to leave you. They loved you very much. They lost you when war came. Don't worry, I will take care of you," I said. "But for now, daylight is coming and we must find a shady place to sleep. We need our strength to cross the border into Ethiopia tomorrow."

I put Chuti down under a tree. He was so tired from crying that he fell right to sleep. As I lay down beside him, I thought of my own parents and how much I missed them.

The following evening we crossed into Ethiopia. Everyone in my group made it. I was proud to be their leader. Other groups were not as lucky. Many boys had died along the way.

The first people we encountered were a small group of women washing clothes in a river. They were surprised to see so many boys all alone and scared.

"Who are these lost boys?" an elderly woman asked.

"We are fleeing war," said one of our leaders.

"You look hungry and sick," another woman said. "We must show you the way to the refugee camp."

"What is a refugee camp?" I asked.

The women told us a refugee camp is a place for people to go when their country is not safe. The kind women stopped their washing and put us on the road to the camp.

In the refugee camp we met a man named Tom who was from the United States. His job was to help refugees like us.

"I will do my best to get you food and shelter," Tom said.

Tom was true to his promise. For the first time in a long while, we ate every day. It wasn't much, just lentils and flour, but after months with almost nothing to eat, it seemed like a feast. We were given tools to build our own mud-and-thatch shelters. To me they were palaces!

We also had the chance to go to school. In the beginning we did not want to go. We wanted to play and forget our hard times. The adults tried to bribe us with cookies, but still many boys did not go to school. The adults became upset with us.

One day a teacher visited me.

"Garang, you must make sure your group comes to school every day," she said. "Education is very important. It can be like your mothers and fathers. It can speak for you in the future, when your parents cannot."

The teacher's words reminded me of how much I missed my parents. I decided to go to school to honor them and to feel they were still with me. My group began to go to school too, even if there were no cookies. English was my favorite subject. We didn't have pencils and paper, so I practiced writing my lessons in the dirt with a stick.

We also learned to pray and worship. Many of us began to go to church every weekend. Faith gave us hope and strength. We began to tell people, "I am not lost. God knows where I am."

Just when it seemed things were finally okay for us, we heard war stirring again. In the distance we saw the flashing lights and heard the terrible thunder. Suddenly there were changes in the camp. Many people began to leave. Soon there was not enough food.

The people of Ethiopia began fighting, and we could not stay in their country anymore. We were chased back to the border of Sudan by war.

It was the rainy season and the huge Gilo River was swollen with water, blocking us from getting to Sudan on the opposite bank. We gathered on the riverbank. Many boys were afraid to enter the river. The current was strong and the rushing water roared like an angry lion. I ordered my group to stay together and to help those who were sick or not strong swimmers.

When we fled the refugee camp, I had taken my schoolbooks with me. As I stood at the river's edge, I decided I would not leave them behind. They were my future—my mother and father.

I tied my schoolbooks around my waist, grabbed Chuti, and jumped into the river. I was so afraid, I don't remember being in the water. I only remember hauling Chuti and myself up onto the opposite bank.

I made sure Chuti was okay, and then waited anxiously for the rest of our group. As boys began to emerge from the river I prayed and counted.

One . . . 12 . . . 22 . . . 27 . . . 31 . . . 35!

We were reunited with everyone in our group—every last one!

We prayed to God to take care of the souls of the brothers we had lost in the river. We also thanked Him for sparing us and prayed for a safe end to our journey.

Later that day, as we prepared for sleep, we saw many big trucks approaching. They were moving very fast, and their rumbling tires sent huge dust clouds into the air. Frightened that there were soldiers in the trucks, we ran to hide.

As the trucks drew closer, my heart began to pound so hard I could hear nothing else. I huddled close to my group, covered my face with my hands, and waited.

After a few minutes I gathered my courage and went to peek through the trees. I saw one of the drivers. It was Tom!

"It's safe, it's safe!" I cried. "Tom has come to save us!"

Many of the boys ran out from the forest, and soon the trucks were surrounded by boys. Everyone wanted to be taken to safety.

Tom began to speak. "I'm very sorry but we cannot take all of you. There is not enough room. For now, we will take only the smallest and those who are too sick to walk. The rest of you must keep walking to Kenya. We will show you the way. Your worst days will soon be behind you."

My group decided that Chuti should go in the truck and the rest of us would walk to Kenya. Chuti wept when I put him in the truck.

"You are leaving me!" Chuti cried.

"No, Chuti," I said, "I am sending you to a safe place. We will join you soon. Until then, you must be strong."

As the trucks drove away, we could see Chuti crying as he watched us through the window. We were sad to see him leave but happy that he would be cared for until we met him in Kenya.

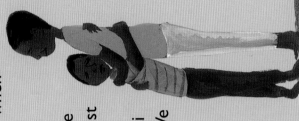

We rejoined the other groups of boys on the road to Kenya. Some parts of the road were well cleared and marked. Others were not. We made sure to keep the trail well marked for the groups behind us.

Many weeks later we made it to a refugee camp in Kenya called Kakuma. There were thousands of people in the camp, but I was determined to find Chuti.

I asked boys from the other groups if they had seen him. One of the leaders told me Tom was taking care of him. Someone showed me to Tom's house, and there I found Chuti eating candy and drawing a picture.

When he saw me, he ran to me and jumped into my arms.

I thanked Tom for taking such good care of Chuti. Then Tom said he needed my help.

"Although you are safe for now, my work is not done," Tom explained. "The war in Sudan is not over, and you and your brothers need to find a place to call home."

"But what can I do?" I asked.

"You must tell me your story—what has happened to you since war came to your country," Tom said. "Your story can help prevent war from creating more lost children, and you can help find a home for yourself and your brothers. Your words will move caring people to help."

So I shared my story with Tom. I talked all day and all night. Then we cried and prayed. After telling my story, the storm of war no longer seemed as scary. The thunder was not as loud.

A few days after our talk, Tom left the camp. Without Tom around, things began to change. Life in Kenya became very hard. There was not enough food. People were often sick and many died.

Some boys in my group became so weak from hunger they could no longer attend school. Then we thought of a way for everyone to get food and education. We took turns foraging for food and going to school. At night the ones who foraged would share their food and the ones who went to school would share their lessons. This way we were able to feed our bodies and our minds.

As I grew older, I tried to improve conditions in the camp. I helped form a drama club and a soccer league so we could have fun things to do. I became a health educator. I taught boys to boil dirty water before drinking it and other ways to prevent sickness.

Chuti was growing older too. I continued to care for him, and he helped me in my work. He was a very smart boy who often tutored other boys in math and English.

I became a young man with responsibilities, which made me feel good. But despite my best efforts, life continued to be a daily struggle for survival. I often worried about my future and Chuti's.

I was twenty-one years old when Tom returned to Kakuma. When I went out to greet him, I almost did not recognize him. His hair had turned gray. I hugged him very hard.

"You have changed, Tom!" I said.

Tom laughed. "Yes, I am now an old man and you are a young man!"

"Where have you been, Tom? Did you forget about us?" I asked.

"I did not forget you, Garang," Tom said. "Your words have been with me, and I have been sharing them with people in many countries. Now the United States is offering you and your brothers a home."

Tom called a meeting and told us about the United States. He said there would be people coming to teach us about this country in preparation for our journey.

I remembered our teachers in Ethiopia telling us that the United States was very far away and life there was very different. I was happy to hear that my brothers and I would have a new place to live, but I was also very afraid. I wondered if people in America would accept me, a lost boy with nothing but a few tattered schoolbooks. I thought it might be better to stay in Kakuma.

I went to the forest to be alone and think about all the things Tom had told us. I also remembered my father's words: Your heart and mind are strong. There is nothing you cannot do.

When I first heard those words, I did not understand them. Now I knew them to be true. My heart was strong with faith and the love of my brothers, and my mind was filled with wisdom from books and the many changes in my life. I was no longer afraid. I would find the strength to make a new life. I would find a new future.

AFTERWORD ▶▶▶▶▶

The Lost Boys' journey took them on a dangerous path across deserts, over mountains, and through rivers. Thousands of the original boys died from the violence, starvation, and diseases they encountered. For others the journey continued to refugee camps, where they lived for years in severe conditions, often existing on one meal a day or less.

In 2000 the United States began its resettlement of approximately 3,800 Lost Boys. These young men, in their early and late twenties, started their lives anew in cities across the United States, from Atlanta, Georgia, to Fargo, North Dakota, and beyond. Before moving to the United States, many of them had never encountered conveniences such as running water, electricity, cars, and modern food preparation. American volunteers helped the Lost Boys in the difficult process of adjusting to their new surroundings and learning the basics of life in a developed country.

Although some of the young men have made tremendous strides in their first few years in the United States, cultural adjustment continues to be a challenge. Several communities of Lost Boys do not benefit from the resources and emotional support of committed volunteers. As a result, some of the young men are finding it difficult to reach their full potential. They struggle to fit in with their American peers, find gainful employment, and access psychological and medical care. Perhaps most frustrating, many of the Lost Boys have had a difficult time accessing and financing the educational opportunities they see as vital to their future and the future of their people.

Despite the numerous challenges they face in the United States, the Lost Boys hold on tightly to their faith and their belief that through education and determination they will one day help bring peace and renewal to their war-torn homeland.

If you wish to learn more about The Lost Boys Foundation, please contact:

The Lost Boys Foundation
100 Auburn Avenue, Suite 200
Atlanta, Georgia 30303
thelbf.org

SUDAN

ETHIOPIA

KENYA

AFRICA